You Are God's Dream

A Collection of Life Giving Affirmations

Kanisha Billingsley

DEDICATION

Dream,

      Your Light infuses the world with peace and love.

        Now go forth and continue to come true!

WithLove-InPeace-ThroughGrace

CONTENTS

INTRODUCTION

Self-love is the starting point of transformative healing. Choose to reconcile with yourself. When one is convinced of her significance and when one is assured of his strength, liberation is possible.

As you read this book, allot time for meditation. Spend time with yourself as you would with a lover. Gaze into your own eyes. Speak the words you desire to hear. Tell your truth(s) without fear of exposure. Write notes filled with love for you.

Invite all of you to heal, to grow, and to be.

I pray that these Words linger within you and around you. I hope these Words call out to you long after the act of reading is complete.

WithLove-InPeace-ThroughGrace,

Kanisha Billingsley

AFFIRMATION 1

I am accepted and embraced.

"Yes you are my Dream—flaws and all!" It is liberating to know that nothing about you diminishes Love's intention for your life. It is empowering to consider that all of you (the imperfect, the great, and the indifferent) constitute the depths of God's Dream.

Now go forth and create the life that calls out for you. Go without shame. Go full of power and confidence.

This is how you come true without compromise

From You to You—A Life Giving Love Note:

_____

_____

_____

_____

_____

_____

_____

_____

_____

_____

_____

_____

_____

_____

From You to You—A Life Giving Love Note:

_____

_____

_____

_____

_____

_____

_____

_____

_____

_____

_____

_____

_____

_____

_____

_____

_____

_____

_____

_____

_____

AFFIRMATION 2

I am emerging full power.

You are emerging...

Every day when you wake and decide to follow Spirit, another dimension of your purpose is born, another volt of your power is released, and another part of you is shared with the world.

Emerging or birthing one's self includes those moments wherein you are not at your best or most healthy. This is being human.

You are emerging...

Be very gentle and gracious with yourself in the process of becoming. New life lessons come when you are equipped to learn them without prejudice and paralysis. The process of discerning, acknowledging, and accepting requires the capacity to fully embody the lessons. Allow your life lessons to take root in your Soul.

This is how you come true without resistance.

From You to You—A Life Giving Love Note:

_____

_____

_____

_____

_____

_____

From You to You—A Life Giving Love Note:

_____

_____

_____

_____

_____

_____

_____

_____

_____

_____

_____

_____

_____

_____

_____

_____

_____

_____

_____

_____

AFFIRMATION 3

I am sufficient.

You are loved and you are of infinite worth. You matter. You matter so much that if you chose to no longer engage your highest self the world would become a bit darker. The sun would not appear to shine the same to the people who know and love you. You matter and you are enough. You are sufficient. You are full of power, purpose, and possibility. You are not alone! You are loved, you are enough, and you are not alone.

Know your worth and honor yourself.

This is how you come true authentically without pretense.

From You to You—A Life Giving Love Note:

_____

_____

_____

_____

_____

_____

_____

_____

_____

_____

_____

From You to You—A Life Giving Love Note:

_____

_____

_____

_____

_____

_____

_____

_____

_____

_____

_____

_____

_____

_____

_____

_____

_____

_____

_____

AFFIRMATION 4

I am intentional about my thoughts and my behaviors.

You are as you intend. At this point in your growth and development, you are the only power that determines who you are. What are your intentions for you and these years you have remaining?

Choose wholeness at all cost. Choose love although the journey is filled with much pain. Choose to surrender to Spirit regardless.

You are as you intend.

This is how you come true without guilt and blame.

From You to You—A Life Giving Love Note:

_____

_____

_____

_____

_____

_____

_____

_____

_____

_____

_____

_____

From You to You—A Life Giving Love Note:

_____

_____

_____

_____

_____

_____

_____

_____

_____

_____

_____

_____

_____

_____

_____

_____

_____

_____

_____

_____

_____

_____

_____

AFFIRMATION 5

I am wise

You make great decisions. When you pause, when you seek truth, and when you listen for Spirit, you make great decisions.

Whatever your decision making process includes do not allow anyone or anything to force you out of your process before you are ready. Pursue wisdom. Pause. Trust your decision making abilities.

In the end, regardless of results, your decision is based on the knowledge and discernment available to you at the time.

Some of your ideas will fail. Failure is not an impeachment of your decision making abilities. Failure indicates success is happening in another form. You make great decisions!

This is how you come true without regrets

From You to You—A Life Giving Love Note:

_____

_____

_____

_____

_____

_____

_____

From You to You—A Life Giving Love Note:

_____

_____

_____

_____

_____

_____

_____

_____

_____

_____

_____

_____

_____

_____

_____

_____

_____

_____

_____

_____

_____

AFFIRMATION 6

I am committed to my personal growth and development.

You must demonstrate that you love yourself and the work you desire to do more than you enjoy repeating unhealthy cycles. The life you desire to live requires more. The next level requires greater depths of surrender.

The requisites for greatness never diminish. Responsibilities and expectations increase to ensure that as you are made visible to the world your entire life can withstand constant exposure to light.

Love who you are and who you desire to be—more.

This is how you come true without self-sabotage.

From You to You—A Life Giving Love Note:

_____

_____

_____

_____

_____

_____

_____

_____

_____

_____

_____

From You to You—A Life Giving Love Note:

_____

_____

_____

_____

_____

_____

_____

_____

_____

_____

_____

_____

_____

_____

_____

_____

_____

_____

_____

_____

AFFIRMATION 7

I am surrendered to The Source and to my highest self.

No matter how much you grind, the number of jobs you have, or the amount of ideas being born within you, the viability of your life and the works of your hands always contend on your willingness to surrender to God. This is true especially when surrendering means not grinding, not working, and not giving.

There are seasons when you must move forward despite uncertainty and trust The Source to provide for you.

There are seasons when surrender means living into an inward focus while developing a more whole self.

Co-create with God, trust your process, surrender, and go forward as Spirit instructs you.

This is how you come true without fear.

From You to You—A Life Giving Love Note:

_____

_____

_____

_____

_____

_____

_____

From You to You—A Life Giving Love Note:

_____

_____

_____

_____

_____

_____

_____

_____

_____

_____

_____

_____

_____

_____

_____

_____

_____

_____

_____

_____

AFFIRMATION 8

I am empowered by self-awareness as I honor my strengths and learn from my struggles.

Sometimes the season of abundance that we desire comes only after an intense period of self-excavating root work.

Perhaps this is your season to become who you need to be for where you desire to go. Who are you? Who are you becoming?

This is how you come true without breaching others.

From You to You—A Life Giving Love Note:

_____

_____

_____

_____

_____

_____

_____

_____

_____

_____

_____

_____

_____

_____

_____

AFFIRMATION 9

I am not seeking perfection.

Choose to become someone who regenerates pain into learning. Choose to become someone who acknowledges her mistakes. Choose to become someone who self-corrects by making another choice. Choose to become someone who does not repeat abusive behaviors or engage abusive thinking.

You were not intended to be perfect. Now forgive yourself and be free.

Release the guilt, shame, and disappointment. Make another emotional choice. Forgive yourself and be.

This is how you come true without self-imprisonment.

From You to You—A Life Giving Love Note:

_____

_____

_____

_____

_____

_____

_____

_____

_____

_____

From You to You—A Life Giving Love Note:

_____

_____

_____

_____

_____

_____

_____

_____

_____

_____

_____

_____

_____

_____

_____

_____

_____

_____

_____

_____

_____

AFFIRMATION 10

I am becoming more authentic.

You will always be in process. You are always becoming more whole and more authentic.

How are you preparing for the life that you want? If you really want [insert the life you want to live] and believe that it is possible, are you prepared for what this life will require of you?

Interrogate your current ways of thinking and being for self-sabotaging tendencies. Do not allow your dreams and ideas to happen upon you and find that you are lacking in preparation. What work (spiritual, emotional, physical, intellectual, and creative) remains undone?

Understanding that perfection is not possible, what assignments call for you now to undergird you then? What do you need to focus on prior to shifting into whatever is next for you?

This is how you come true without procrastination.

From You to You—A Life Giving Love Note:

_____

_____

_____

_____

_____

_____

From You to You—A Life Giving Love Note:

_____

_____

_____

_____

_____

_____

_____

_____

_____

_____

_____

_____

_____

_____

_____

_____

_____

_____

_____

_____

_____

_____

AFFIRMATION 11

I am enough.

You are Light. Who you are at your core precludes your Light from dimming. You are always bright even on your worst day. You are Light because you choose to remain connected to The Source.

Now go forth bright and shine/ shine/ shine as you come true again and again!!!

This is how you come true without self-condemnation.

From You to You—A Life Giving Love Note:

_____

_____

_____

_____

_____

_____

_____

_____

_____

_____

_____

_____

_____

_____

From You to You—A Life Giving Love Note:

_____

_____

_____

_____

_____

_____

_____

_____

_____

_____

_____

_____

_____

_____

_____

_____

_____

_____

_____

_____

_____

AFFIRMATION 12

I am life giving.

Attempting to repress your Light is like putting a band-aid on an erupting volcano. No amount of bandages can hide who you are now. And like the volcano, whatever is within you seeps out and covers everything in its path. Do not resist, do not hide, and do not run because in the end you will erupt.

The quality of what pours forth from you is determined by the small details of your daily life.

This is how you come true without unnecessary tension.

From You to You—A Life Giving Love Note:

_____

_____

_____

_____

_____

_____

_____

_____

_____

_____

_____

From You to You—A Life Giving Love Note:

_____

_____

_____

_____

_____

_____

_____

_____

_____

_____

_____

_____

_____

_____

_____

_____

_____

_____

_____

_____

_____

_____

_____

AFFIRMATION 13

I am in love with myself.

Choose to surrender to your highest most whole self. Let her be born now. Crossroads are not intended to last forever. A decision has to be made.

Choose to love yourself and who you will be more than anything or anyone that you fear. In all your ways, honor your commitments to The Source and to your highest self.

This is how you come true without co-dependency.

From You to You—A Life Giving Love Note:

_____

_____

_____

_____

_____

_____

_____

_____

_____

_____

_____

_____

_____

_____

_____

AFFIRMATION 14

I am capable.

[It] is not going to be easy but [it] is possible. You can do [it]! Whatever [it] is—you can, you should, and you will with a lot of discipline and wisdom. Remember, [it] and you are possible!!!

This is how you come true without doubt.

From You to You—A Life Giving Love Note:

_____

_____

_____

_____

_____

_____

_____

_____

_____

_____

_____

_____

_____

_____

_____

_____

_____

AFFIRMATION 15

I am courageous.

You have come true in some areas of your life. The next leg of your journey is going to require an expanded consciousness, deeper spiritual connection, and greater self-awareness. This three strand chord is only efficacious when you choose to believe beyond your fears.

Believe beyond your fears associated with acceptance and abandonment. Believe beyond your fears associated with love and expressed sacred sexual energy. Believe beyond your fears associated with being and becoming.

This is how your coming true liberates others.

From You to You—A Life Giving Love Note:

_____

_____

_____

_____

_____

_____

_____

_____

_____

_____

_____

From You to You—A Life Giving Love Note:

_____

_____

_____

_____

_____

_____

_____

_____

_____

_____

_____

_____

_____

_____

_____

_____

_____

_____

_____

_____

AFFIRMATION 16

I am safe.

Every resource that I need surrounds me.

It is impossible to secure everything at all times. You will lose things along the way. Grace is the return of all that remains vital to your current vibration and intentions.

What was once lost is now found again...

Trust that what you have at this present moment is all that you need.

This is how you come true without anxiety and worry.

From You to You—A Life Giving Love Note:

_____

_____

_____

_____

_____

_____

_____

_____

_____

_____

_____

_____

_____

AFFIRMATION 17

I am open to new people and to new experiences.

Your imagination, your dreams, your desires, your intuition, and Spirit journeyed with you through previous endeavors. Now perhaps it is time to dream another dream.

In life you will experience multiple free spaces wherein you are not where you were and you have not reached your next step. In these spaces, regardless of your age, you are able to create new ideas and to pursue new dreams. Do not despise your free spaces; instead, celebrate that you are not shackled to former ways of thinking and being.

Purpose is not a solitary destination that we reach over the course of our lifetime. Purpose is a journey to many different places with many different people who are in need of your passion.

Dare to dream again!

This is how you come true without stagnation.

From You to You—A Life Giving Love Note:

_____

_____

_____

_____

_____

_____

From You to You—A Life Giving Love Note:

_____

_____

_____

_____

_____

_____

_____

_____

_____

_____

_____

_____

_____

_____

_____

_____

_____

_____

_____

_____

AFFIRMATION 18

I am Divine artistic expression.

You are beautiful—breathtakingly beautiful [PERIOD]! Everything about you is divine artist expression—you are beautiful.

Accepting your acceptance and honoring your quirky, unique, and strange beauty is how you come true conscious of yourself without being self-conscious.

You are beautiful—breathtakingly beautiful [PERIOD]!

From You to You—A Life Giving Love Note:

_____

_____

_____

_____

_____

_____

_____

_____

_____

_____

_____

_____

_____

_____

AFFIRMATION 19

I am responsible and trustworthy.

There is power in self-affirmation. The ability to wrestle a glimmer of light from within one's own internal darkness is what undergirds revolutionaries. Calling yourself forward following periods of external resistance and defeat is the first level perfected by many people. The most difficult aspect of self-love is having the strength to affirm the self after periods of self-sabotaging behaviors. When one is most weak in her humanity, her own willingness to forgive, to call forth her healing, and to push to her highest self distinguishes her.

Seasons will surely come when the only sounds that will pull you forward are the cries of your own Soul. Seasons will surely come when the only encouragement available is what you offer to yourself. Seasons will surely come when the only joy you experience is the joy you create.

Now go forth as an advocate for your wholeness. Go forth as one who affirms her immeasurable worth and infinite value regardless.

This is what it means to come true!

From You to You—A Life Giving Love Note:

_____

_____

_____

_____

From You to You—A Life Giving Love Note:

_____

_____

_____

_____

_____

_____

_____

_____

_____

_____

_____

_____

_____

_____

_____

_____

_____

_____

_____

AFFIRMATION 20

I am coming true…

You are loved. You are accepted. You are wanted. You are needed. You are necessary. You are irreplaceable. You are God's DreamSeed!

If someone took the time to construct a perfected image of a human being in their mind, this image would pale in comparison to you. You are the dream only God could conceive. You, Beloved, are the one only Spirit could bring forth.

Thank you for choosing to come true in your own heart, mind, and soul. Now, go forth as God's Dream and choose to exist in the world as transformative revolutionary love!

From You to You—A Life Giving Love Note:

_____

_____

_____

_____

_____

_____

_____

_____

_____

_____

From You to You—A Life Giving Love Note:

_____

_____

_____

_____

_____

_____

_____

_____

_____

_____

_____

_____

_____

_____

_____

_____

_____

_____

_____

_____

_____

_____

Were you inspired by this collection of affirmations? Share your story by emailing me at: rev.kanisha@kanishabillingsley.com.

I look forward to hearing from you!

ABOUT THE AUTHOR

Kanisha Billingsley is a writer, minister, and author of the inspirational email devotional series, *A Life Giving Moment*. She lives with her husband in Atlanta, Ga. For more information about her upcoming publications, events, preaching engagements, and to subscribe to the *A Life Giving Moment* journey, please visit www.kanishabillingsley.com.

* 9 7 8 0 6 1 5 9 4 7 4 4 0 *